SHORTCUT TO FIXING A COMPUTER

How to Repair A Computer In 24 Hours or Less !

Brandon Ragoo

CONTENTS

Title Page	1
Introduction	4
CHAPTER 1: Common Computer Problems And Quick Fixes	6
CHAPTER 2: Understanding How A Computer Works	12
CHAPTER 3: Testing the main hardware components	15
CHAPTER 4: Repair and Reinstall operating system	20
CHAPTER 5: Preventing Future Issues	24
Conclusion	28

INTRODUCTION

Over the past 10 years I've constantly seen and met many IT professionals who have all the paper work to be qualified and even years of experience in the field (some even more than me) that simply don't understand how to fix a computer. They simply don't understand how a computer works. IT managers, technicians, students and even worst of all teachers, the same teachers who could be teaching your kids IT, are completely clueless on getting a computer to work as it should. The sad reality is those teachers or managers are the ones the students or interns learn from or look up to and it results in the new generation not being able to accomplish the task they were required to accomplish at their job. It's a process which repeats itself while I wright this book and one day I hope this book can help chance that, one day I hope this book can help change the world. My name is Brandon Ragoo, and I have been an IT professional for ten years ongoing. I have both the paper work and years experience in the work environment to qualify as a professional, join me while I guide you through the process of repairing any computer within 24 hours.

This book was written and specifically designed to help anyone, even a complete computer novice on how to repair any computer. With that being said, while it does provide the steps and information necessary, I'm not going to be holding your hand step by step and walking you through the process, as I believe it's a complete waste of time and if you can't put in the extra effort to complete the task at hand, then you may never reach far in life, as you need to have the desire and will power in order to accomplish your goals in life. At least that's the way I was thought. For example in this book I mentioned about booting from Hiren's bootable CD or a Windows DVD to repair a computer, I'm not going to walk you through the step by step process of downloading and creating this DVD. There are many YouTube videos and articles on Google on how to do this, it's a complete waste of time going through this process, use the resources at hand. If you don't know what RAM is Google it or simply watch a YouTube video on removing a RAM stick if you're too lazy to read an article. If you don't like my method of teaching fine, go back to school or find another IT professional to teach you (if he even knows IT) what I'm about to teach you, but I guarantee, they can't teach it the way I do. At least most can't.

This book consist of five chapters, the first chapter is for those who just want to fix the problem as fast as possible and continue with their day, the second explains how computers work, the third explains how to test hardware components, the fourth talks about repairing and reinstalling the operating system while the final chapter talks about preventing future issues. Do with these chapters as you will but remember as Peter Parker once said in the comics "With Great Power Comes Great Responsibility".

CHAPTER 1: COMMON COMPUTER PROBLEMS AND QUICK FIXES

CHAPTER 1: Common Computer Problems And Quick Fixes

◆ ◆ ◆

Computer won't power on

1. Check to ensure all cables are connected and not slack or disconnected.
- Sometimes cables may get slack or unplugged by accident. It can save a lot of time by checking the simple things first.

2. Check to ensure the outlet is providing power.
- You can check this by simply plugging in another device such as a fan or cell phone charger.

3. Test the power supply.
- If you're using a Dell desktop there is sometimes a tiny black button located at the back of the power supply that you can press to test the power supply. If when pressed and the light behind the power supply turns green the power supply is good, if not the power supply bad.
- If you are using a custom built desktop or any other desktop you have to use a power supply tester or multi meter. If the power supply test passes then unfortunately the motherboard is bad and needs to be replaced. If the power supply test fails the power supply needs to be replaced.
- If you're using a laptop, simply switch the power adapter with one that you are positive works or use a multi meter. If the power adapter is bad simply replace. If the power adapter is good then unfortunately the motherboard or charging port needs to be replaced.

No display on monitor

1. Check to ensure all cables are connected and not slack or disconnected
2. Drain all power from the desktop computer by doing the following steps:
   - Disconnect the power cable from behind the desktop tower
   - Hold down the power button for 30 seconds
   - Release the power button and reconnect the power cable
   - Power on the desktop
3. Reseat the RAM.
   - Remove the RAM sticks from inside the desktop tower
   - Repeat step 2.
   - Reinsert the RAM (if more than one stick insert one stick at a time also try different RAM slots)
   - Power on the desktop
   - Replace monitor (if no spare monitor try all other steps first or connect the monitor to another device to test monitor)
4. Removal of graphic card (if using dedicated graphic card)
   - Remove the dedicated graphic card and reconnect to the integrated VGA (or any other display port).
   - Reset computer BIOS (remove CMOS) battery for 2 minutes
   - Restart the computer

If still no display the motherboard is bad and needs to be replaced.

Can't get to Windows login screen

1. Boot into safe mode
   - If using an older operating system such as Windows XP or Windows 7 you can simply get into safe mode constantly

hitting F8 on the keyboard immediately after pressing the power button, until the option appears for safe mode. If the same issue occurs with safe mode proceed to step 2. If it does not occur proceed to step 4.

2. Repair Windows boot manager
   - To repair Windows boot manager you can either allow Windows to atomically repair the boot manager (option given when in proper shutdown occurred) or boot from a Windows bootable media and use command prompt.

3. Replace the hard drive
   - In most causes if the Windows files are corrupted and can't be repaired the hard drive will need to be replaced. Once a new hard drive is replaced Windows will need to be installed on the new hard drive

4. Video Drivers
   - If you were able to successfully boot into safe mode then Windows video driver may have been the issue. You can try removing, rollback to old version or install the latest version of the video driver to rectify the issue. You can also simply do a system restore to a day and time when the computer worked without any issues.

Forgot computer password or can't login

1. Boot into safe mode (see "Can't get to Windows login screen" step 1 one how to do this).
   - If successfully able to login to safe mode proceed to step 3 if not proceed to step 2.

2. Boot into Hirens Bootable CD
   - If unable to successfully login in safe mode then you most likely had forgotten your password. You can simply remove your password using Hirens Bootable CD.

3. Perform a system restore to a day and time when you were able to login.

Performance issues or delayed startup time

1. Disable unnecessary startup applications
   - While many articles will mention using MSCONFIG to perform this task I personally recommend you use a program (free) named "Autoruns" to accomplish the task. You can also use both. Be sure to create a system restore point before making changes to startup applications if you're not a computer expert.

2. Check resource usage
   - Some computers especially the cheap computers are simply not built to handle more than simply typing a word document or doing research online. Check your resource usage using task manager to determine if the usage is high. If RAM usage is high simply upgrade RAM if its CPU usage it's better to replace the computer.

3. Hard Drive failure
   - If both task above failed to rectify the issue then it may be the hard drive starting to fail if not bad already. A hard drive (mechanical) usually last five years before starting to fail. Replace the hard drive and even consider getting an SSD (Solid State Drive) for better performance (less storage).

Computer atomically shuts down

1. Test power supply and check connections
   - Follow the first three steps in "Computer won't power on" before proceeding further.

2. Boot into the BIOS and leave computer power on.
- If automatic shutdown still occurs overheating may be the issue, if it does not occur replace hard drive.

3. Overheating
- If the system did shutdown while in BIOS overheating may be the issue. Remove all dust from inside your desktop or laptop using compressed air. It is also recommended to remove and reapply thermal compound to the CPU.

Virus Removal

1. Boot into Linux Distro
- If your system does unfortunately become infected with a virus I recommend you immediately shutdown your system and boot into a Linux distro to manually copy data (at least the important files) to a flash drive or external hard drive.

2. Boot into Hirens Bootable CD
- Boot into Hiren's Bootable CD (choose mini Windows XP from the menu) and remove all infections using malware bytes.

3. Perform second scan in safe mode
- Once malware bytes is complete, boot Windows into safe mode and perform a second scan using AVG or Avast.

4. Reinstall Windows
- If after both methods were performed the system is still showing signs of infection, a reinstall is the only option left.

CHAPTER 2: UNDERSTANDING HOW A COMPUTER WORKS

CHAPTER 2: Understanding How A Computer Works

❖ ❖ ❖

How does the computer work?

To keep it simple a computer requires an input in order to produce an output. The computer will receive the input from an input device such as a mouse or keyboard, process the data received and output the data through an output device such as a monitor or printer. A computer consist of five basic components,

Motherboard, CPU (Central Processing Unit), RAM (Random Access Memory), Hard Drive and Power Supply. Each of these components a described below.

Basic components inside a computer

1. Motherboard – A motherboard is basically a large circuit board inside a computer which all the components connect to. This motherboard enables components to communicate with each other as it is used to transfer data from one component to the next.
2. CPU – The CPU (Central Processing Unit) which is sometimes called the processor, performs all mathematical calculations inside a computer. It is basically the brain of the computer.
3. RAM – RAM (Random Access Memory) is volatile memory. Volatile memory means that it was designed to only store data while the computer is powered on. Once the computer is powered off the data will be gone.
4. Hard Drive – The hard drive contains non-volatile mem-

ory. This is the opposite of volatile memory which means weather the computer is powered on or off the memory remains stored on the device.
5. Power Supply – The power supply simply provides power to the computer and all its internal components by converting AC into DC current. A power adapter does this for a laptop.

The operating system

The operating system is the software installed onto the hard drive which you see when the computer is powered on. Windows 7, Mac OS, Android and Linux Mint are examples of operating systems. The operating system is what enables humans to interact with the computer. The operating system will consist of drivers which enables it to recognize and communicate with a computer's internal hardware components and external devices such as printers. Without drivers the operating system simply can't identify the device which is why printers and dedicated graphic cards for example come included with drivers.

CHAPTER 3: TESTING THE MAIN HARDWARE COMPONENTS

CHAPTER 3: Testing The Main Hardware Components

❖ ❖ ❖

Testing the power supply

 1. *Dell power supply self-test*
    - *Most Dell desktops come with a small black button behind the power supply which is used for testing. If when pressed the light (also behind the power supply) turns green the power supply is good. If it does not turn green the power supply is bad and should be replaced.*

 2. *Standard power supply test*
    - *If you're desktop consist of a standard power supply that does not have a self-test button simply use a power supply tester or multi meter.*
    - *If you don't have a power supply tester or multi meter you can also use a spare (once you are confident it is working) or new power supply to confirm whether the existing one is bad.*

Testing the hard drive

 1. *Hard Drive testing software*
    - *Boot into Hirens Bootable CD or ultimate boot CD (select hard drive diagnostic from the menu) and select the appropriate hard drive test, for example if you have a Segate hard drive select the hard drive test for Segate, if you have a western digital hard drive select "Data Lifeguard Diagnostics". If*

SHORTCUT TO FIXING COMPUTERS

you are unsure what brand hard drive you have be sure to open your desktop or laptop to check or you can check the model in the BIOS. Once the model is found a simple Google search with the model number will give you the hard drive manufacturer. It is recommended to do a full hard drive test.

2. *CHKDSK*
- *Many books and articles will mention using chkdsk or third party utilities, however I found third party utilities to be unreliable and chkdsk only used when files need to be repaired on a hard drive in good condition as repairing files on a bad hard drive (if it even can be repaired) will just be a temporary fix.*

3. *Replace hard drive if at least 5 years old*
- *Once a hard drive is at least 5 years old and the system is performing slow I will recommend replacing the hard drive as based on experienced although the test may pass hard drives start to decrease in performance after five years.*

Testing the RAM (Random Access Memory)

1. *Windows Memory Diagnostic*
- *Boot into Hirens or Ultimate Boot CD and select Windows Memory Diagnostic. Press the letter T on the keyboard to perform a long test. You can also find this utility included in Windows 7 or more recent operating systems.*

2. *Swap Memory*
- *If you are confident memory is bad or don't want to wait to perform a full memory test simply swap the memory with another compatible working stick of RAM, however in my experience it is very uncommon for memory to go bad.*

3. Try another RAM slot
- A lot of times when a motherboard is starting to fail the RAM slot may malfunction causing technicians to think the memory stick is faulty. Try another RAM slot and see if the same issue occurs

Testing the motherboard

1. Inspect the motherboard
- Simply take a close look at the motherboard use a magnifying glass if you need to and see if any capacitors are leaking or chips are damaged.

2. Look for signs of motherboard failure
- While there are no software designed for testing motherboards or hardware devices that are actually reliable in testing motherboards looking for simple signs of failure can be enough to determine motherboard failure. Some signs of motherboard failure are USB (back ports) malfunction, RAM slot malfunction, no video display and system will only power on at random times or power needs to be drained from the board (disconnecting the power cable and holding down power button for 30 seconds) before the computer can power on.

3. Test all other major hardware components (except CPU)
- It is recommended that before declaring motherboard failure that all other major hardware components be tested (you can ignore CPU test) as well as the two previous steps mentioned.

Testing the CPU

1. CPU testing software
- While there are software designed by the manufacturer such as "Intel Processor Diagnostic Tool" and many third party

programs you can find online to test the CPU, I honestly in my ten years studying and working as an IT technician have never seen the need to use these tools as all other components will fail before the CPU fails if it even does fail.

1. Swap the CPU
- *If you however have any reason the believe the CPU is bad or will like to test it just to confirm simply swap the CPU with another CPU which is the same exact model or atleast compatible with the CPU socket.*

Testing OEM (original equipment manufacturer) computers

It is worth mentioning that although the information given above can be used to test all hardware components, OEM computers such as Dell come with preinstalled diagnostic software which can be used to test all hardware components or at least the major components. This software can be accessed by constantly tapping a key on the keyboard the moment the computer is powered on, such as F12 for example.

CHAPTER 4: REPAIR AND REINSTALL OPERATING SYSTEM

CHAPTER 4: Repair and Reinstall operating system

❖ ❖ ❖

Repairing the boot manager or operating system

1. Windows XP repair
- To repair Windows XP boot manager or operating system repaired one is required to boot from a Windows XP disk and select the option to repair Windows XP.

2. Windows Vista, 7, 8.1 and 10 repair
- Since the release of Windows Vista the operating systems were designed to atomically repair themselves if an improper shutdown occurred causing files to get corrupted. If however the automatic repair fails you will be given the advanced options such as to repair using command prompt or even attempting to perform a system restore. You can try both those methods and see which once works for you. Windows 10 does however offer the options to reset the operating system while keeping the data (only third party programs removed) but I will always recommended to back up your data sill as if this process fails data loss can occur.

Backing up data and reinstalling the operating system

1. Using a bootable Linux distro
- You can manually copy and paste the files from your hard

drive to an external hard drive by booting into a Linux distro such as Ubuntu or Linux mint. The Linux distro will be loaded into RAM and will not affect any data on your hard drive. Once done the operating system can be reinstalled using the Windows DVD or if you're using Windows 10 there should be an option to reset Windows 10 which will erase all data and programs (third party). This is basically a factory reset of Windows 10.

2. *Using a hard drive docking station, USB to SATA/IDE data cable or simply connecting the hard drive in another desktop as a slave.*
   - *There are two devices which are available that every computer technician should have, a hard drive docking station and a USB to SATA data cable. The hard drive docking station works by simply allowing you to stick the hard drive into the slot provided and connect a USB cable to a desktop or laptop. This will allow you to copy data from the hard drive. The USB to SATA/IDE data cable works by connecting one end to the hard drive and the other end (USB) to a desktop or laptop. You can then copy data from the hard drive. The final method will be to connect the hard drive inside a desktop as a slave and copy the data from the hard drive. Whichever method you choose or is available to you, once done you can boot from your Windows 10 disk to reinstall Windows or simply factory reset Windows 10.*

3. *System Clone or hard drive image*
   - *There is a more advanced method of backing up data which is cloning the hard drive or created a system image (snapshot). The method can be done using a third party program named "Macrium Reflect" however this method will be described in more detail in another book as it is not recommended for beginners.*

Restore data and reinstall programs

1. Manually copy data
   - Once the reinstall of Windows was successful (be sure to install all drivers needed) you can simply copy and paste data from external hard drive or flash drive to your hard drive again. Once done you can begin reinstalling programs.

2. Restore hard drive clone or system image
   - If the more advanced method was done which is a system clone or hard drive image this can be restored by simply installing the new hard drive (if a clone was done) or copying the image to the hard drive and using Macrium Reflect to mount the image and extract the data. Once done programs can be reinstalled (if it was a clone no need to reinstall programs).

CHAPTER 5: PREVENTING FUTURE ISSUES

CHAPTER 5: Preventing Future Issues

❖ ❖ ❖

Create Restore Points

1. Creating a system restore point
- System restore points are one of the best ways to prevent downtime whenever a software related issue occurs such as a bad Windows update which may cause the system to malfunction. This feature is enabled by default on Windows XP however on more modern operating systems such as Windows 10 you may have to manually enable this feature. Once done it is recommended to create a restore point once the computer is working well and before any changes are made to the system. For example it is wise to create a restore point before installing a new program to test or updating your video drivers.

Configure Windows Updates

1. Set a time to install updates
- Windows can be configured to install Windows updates at a specific date and time. This can be done to prevent Windows from atomically restarting your system at times when you need to use your system immediately and also prevent downtime as you can set the updates to install at a specific date and time where you will have the time to not only create a restore point before but also test and ensure no issues occurred after the update. Windows does however atomically create a restore point before installing updates. Windows 10 in-

cluded a new feature where you can even have more control over updates and set active hours so updates will not attempt to install during those hours.

2. Disable Windows Updates
- Windows updates can be disabled on Windows (not Windows 10) by simply going to the list of services and disabling Windows updates. Although Windows updates is known to cause problems at times, it is recommended to install all Windows updates are many of the updates are bug fixes and security updates for vulnerabilities found in Windows.

Virus Protection

1. Installing an antivirus program
- Unless you're using a server, a free antivirus such as AVG or Avast is enough to keep your computer protected.

2. HTTPS and Adblock addon
- If you're using Google Chrome or Mozilla FireFox which you should simply installing the addons HTTPS everywhere and adblock can help protect you system from getting viruses.

3. Be Cautious
- You can have the best and most expensive antivirus in the word and the best firewall, if you do not be cautious and pay attention to what you download or open online you can risk getting your desktop infected. Be sure to not visit any unknown websites to download any files. If you are unsure about the website do some research on the website first.

Automatic Backups

1. Second Copy
- Second Copy can be download for free (trial 30 days) and

once installed this can be configured to back up your desktop daily. This can back up your desktop to either a network location or simply a flash drive. Even if the 30 day trial expires, the automatic backups will still run at the scheduled day and time.

CONCLUSION

So by now you know, repairing a computer is not rocket science and it's clearly not as complicated as school books make it sound or the fake IT professionals make it sound by using technical terms just to sound smart and complicated. Any computer desktop, laptop or server can be repaired in 24 hours. Use the information I provided,, study it, medicate on it and go out there and be one of the best technicians the world has to offer, but remember as I said before "with great power comes great responsibility".

Made in the USA
Coppell, TX
05 February 2020